Embracing the Moment

Embracing the Moment
Copyright @2016 by Michael E. Belongie. All rights reserved.

No part of this publication may be reproduced or transmitted
in any way without the express written consent of the author.

Published by Little Dane Girl Press

Cover Design by Karla R. Jensen and Rodney Schroeter
Artist Agent/Designer Karla R. Jensen
Jr. Copy Editor Meredith T. Zimmermann
Original Artwork by Anne Christian
Back page poet photo by Mary Schoenfeld and artist photo by Mark
Weller, with permissions granted.

Published in the United States of America
ISBN: 978-0-9967194-4-5
Nonfiction/Poetry

About the front cover photo:
Grandchild and Golden Retriever, Keats

Embracing the Moment

Michael E. Belongie

Artist and Illustrator
Anne Christian

Previous Collections
By Michael E. Belongie

Kinship with the Stars
These Kindred Stars
As Ancient as Stars
All Things Living, Mighty & Small
Now Is All We Have
Beckoned By The Star Maker

Past collaborations have included and benefited Holy Wisdom Monastery, Beaver Dam Area Arts Association and Green Lake Conference Center.

Embracing the Moment, my seventh poetry chapbook, reflects a contemplative response to daily living somewhat less-harried and respectful of waning opportunities to embrace all with youthful energies. Quieting allows enlightenment- a toddler grandchild reaching out to her golden retriever - each nurtured.

There can be no exclusionary strictures about what constitutes the contemplative. Neither creed nor mindfulness ensures enrollment. Numerous poems attend to a singularity of an event notably recognized in a refreshing, illumining and ascending moment.

With warm welcome, gather yourself and allow that sublime to awaken within.

Michael Belongie

PART ONE:

Embracing the Moment

Wellspring	2
Is that so?	2
Suffer we do or suffer we must?	3
Solstice	3
Trapped	4
For Love	4
Birthday Monday	5
Tarry and Away	6
A New World's View	7
Whencesover	8
And This Too Shall Pass	9
Wafting	10
Ten Will Get Twenty	11
In Surrender	12

Part One:

Embracing the Moment

Wellspring

That moment as golden retriever,
Keats, embracing the moment
of infant granddaughter on her back,
fingers enfolding its snout.

The resulting licks,
her maternal bonding,
the elemental parsed
with syllables of love.

Is that so?

Lifting veils
inward we
hone our hearts
to realize the holy.

Suffer we do or suffer we must?

Daylight or darkening into night, the stand-alone mind is tipped and domino effect topples brick onto brick. Spiraling in twist and turns, be it downturn in health, reverse in fortune, ceasing of the living. A pattern upended, removed. Sorting and gathering, each brick; should we realign from memory or begin another?

Solstice

The teen-age clerk hands me
the receipt, a senior discount
inserted. Recalibrate stopwatch.

Trapped

Glossed-over eyes,
captive audience
darts exits.

For Love

> "More torturous than all else is the human heart,
> beyond remedy, who can understand it."
> *Jeremiah 17:9*

Roiled ocean, miles deep
we will to be adrift, faltering;
azimuth charted.
Hold a course, naive;
each navigates; extraneous
hearts, we languish.
One with the sea and each other,
ferment and foam, its oxygen
air pockets shared.
And our time to tread, swim,
bob, flounder, surrender.

Birthday Monday

In a sixtieth cycle
we celebrate a
final offspring;
for a farmer's daughter
an aged mother's care-giver.

A nurse, a wife, a football
fan, and mother, a coach
blended and folded
into cakes, cookies and bread.

Stand in the wind, rain,
never one to shelter with
umbrella, take the elements;
less we dawdle.

Care, the measure of a heart
set in motion; rest a measure
then forward, later take stock
of love's return.

Tarry and Away

Such sport and fancy to portray Oberon
in Britten's Midsummer Night's Dream.
And half the country away we await
the accolades assured to follow.
This summer's ripeness and woodland
canopy surround the Wolftrap venue.
That world's all-a-stage elixir, your psyche
imbibed with toddler's prattle.
Such sweet and sad separation as
we intuit and relish a gift to be
shared and lavished in effervescent
breath and heft of operatic.
Love and light, dream and world
await, we tarry and then away.

*Ryan, our son, was performing with the Wolf Trapp Opera Company, Washington D.C.

A New World's View

Not a vale for tears,
this here and now,
rather the realm for mercy.
We are not to languish;
avoid the jagged edge,
extremes with fire and ice.
Each transverses
sedimentary layers,
teeming with life's protein.
Tubers await ripeness
and resurrections with
seasonal rotation.
And tears, our liquid soul,
christen and anoint.

Whencesoever

Our own nano-second world
is ours for tending, whence
to know how we are
to revere, prune, or alter
creation about this garden.

And This Too Shall Pass

Out of the wide and narrow window
past midnight, the thirty-foot tops
of arborvitae sway.

I recall those towering
specimens planted in a
staggered line for privacy,

requested at planting
six feet in height, gifted
to us from mother-in-law.

This wintry night, wife asleep,
her mother passed,
and two sons variously relocated,
I am comforted.

Arborvitae stretch higher,
heedless to expending sap
outward and upward.

Yet this night, my solitary
witness finds consolation
in surrender to windy buffets.

So many nights we resist,
anxious, a nightly ritual
of just letting go.

Wafting

In the idiom of language,
"I'm hangin' on by a thread;"
plodding about the protracted
drifts of snow's topography.

The threads unraveling
goad most to eclipse
the here and now, abdicate
saintly surrender.

"I cannot let go," a supposition
of self-centered control
that outflanks a needed
descent and deferring.

The clipped winged
so often and sorely flutters,
not wafts in air.

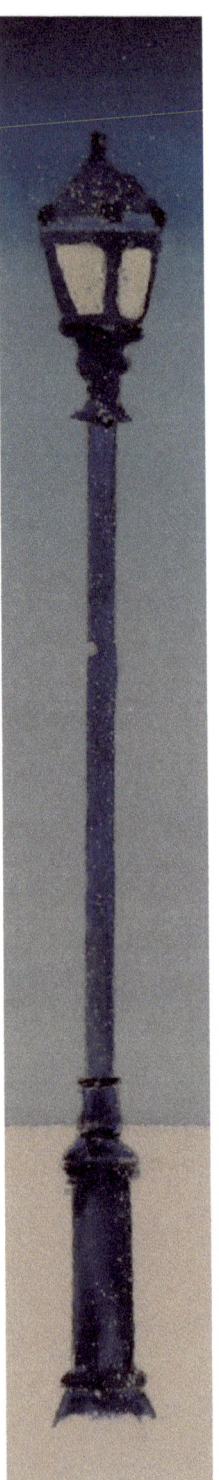

Ten Will Get Twenty

Opening a bureau drawer in bedroom
I sort through and discover Mother's
last Christmas card, signed, though blind
except for orbs of light; from
rote her unmistakable Palmer script.

And the two ten dollar bills, crisp
and uncirculated I recall; I just could
not part with; here they are, anchored
with tape as three years have
come and gone, and I hold resolve.

Letting go of a thousand flash points
of roiling emotions, filtered through
holidays shared with neverland
whims and dreams upend
my wit to spend the cash.

Practical and poetic teeter;
what's twenty in this topsy-turvy?
It's not her legacy just a two note
shorthand, there's more to it
than, "Love and hugs, Mom."

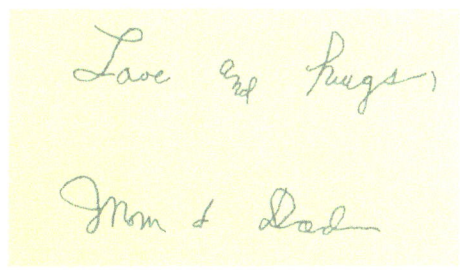

In Surrender

Even in the ordinary,
coarse-ground pepper
in glass shaker,
even grasp, anticipating
pungent accent, celebrate.

Take pause in blizzard's
fury, batten unanchored,
hold resolve indoors,
stay its course.

Trifle and tragedy,
just trajectory and force,
mete the consequences
in our own forbearing.

PART TWO:

Interface in the Human Shuffle

Leave-taking	14
Google for the Story	15
Luminous Currency	16
Irrelevancy	17
Relevancy, Companion Poem	17
Dream Song	18
San Francisco Post	18
Unholy Times	19
Barefoot and Buckshot	20
A Dream Missive	21
Winter Solstice	21
We Are Driftwood	22

Part Two

Interface in the Human Shuffle

Leave-taking

Fifty-one e-mails remain not
relegated to the trash;
each eek out meaning with
ongoing interactions.

Key words are perused
"I will send the check to you.
Become an Eco Volunteer.
Excellent article on Haiti."
A puzzler: do e-mails languish
until newer ones appear?
Delete when check clears,
article is read and you volunteer.
Electronic messaging and leave-
taking interface in human shuffle.

Google for the Story

The template is familiar —
input the germane key words:
Lutheran minister and hit and run.
Articles; indices outline
arraignment, bond, entering treatment,
referencing news through sentencing.
Absent: fatality scene, a memorial of
victim's running shoes at crosswalk
evokes stupendous loss and pain
Funeral and families entombed:
grief, sorrow, losses entwined in a wreath
that evokes the Good Friday refrain.

Luminous Currency
Halloween Eve

Imagine seven billion humans
whirring in miasmic consciousness,
the promise for Jacob's descendants.

Grant Merton's grace to enfold
this teeming agape of bodies and
spirits without boundaries.

Steward phosphorous, a precious
currency, to abate starvation in
this fertile blue-green orb.

Labor we all in infinite possibilities
that we are within the divine.

Irrelevancy

There is no threat to bear with -
in the hawk's talons, rending the
feathers of unsuspecting prey.

The protest so short, the shrill
squawk piercing, collision
calculating this token trophy.
Irrelevant that mindfulness
usurps vain startle.

Relevancy, Companion Poem

Hawk's wing span
outstretched, vulnerable
from above.

Agitated pecking of sparrows,
swoop upon swoop;
miscalculated territory.
The invasion follows
tit for tat.

References Wisconsin's only recall election.

Dream Song

Dreams, attend to them
awake and re-enter the
other world terrains, sub-
conscious subterfuges.

Dreams, surrender
nightly as we mend
mind and heart while on
this sleep odyssey.

Dreams, enroll with fantastical
casts of thousands searching
on this upended stage,
hidden epiphany.

Dreams, reverence with much ado our
child's heart; and as we draw toward
doom and dread hold
at bay a bolting retreat.

San Francisco Post

With fault line and lore of gold, juxtaposed divide,
endemic homeless habituate Market Street. A Reagan
boondoggle to rend kinship; shift for themselves:
the unhinged, unemployable, untenanted. Shifting
platelets, reactive again and again; ordinances enacted;
refit societal towers to be quake ready. An ever-
altering teeter-totter of have and have-nots. Awaiting.

Unholy Times

Muddling through this mild winter,
infrequent snow, abnormal warmth
geese have crisscrossed skies.

Great Recession and political cacophony
wink and blink and blare in stridency
salvos amid unemployed, homeless.

The disenchanted of this global village
have heightened appetite; thirty four
million iPhone to satiate unholy demand.

America's nine-percent unemployed
circle uncertain, yearning for safe harbor.

Barefoot and Buckshot

The dream is revisited
in a parallel farm house,
Jon's kitchen is entered.

Larger group is milling
about as sliding pocket
doors open to people
performing yoga-like
movements.

I watch, engaged
though standoffish.

Metaphor in a young
boy sprinkling bird shot
on the worn, wooden
floor as if seeding a field.

Taken aback, I enunciate,
"Stop this; can't they
see the danger?"

A Dream Missive

Two golden velour pillows
request a poem, a pause
with Sabbath solemn chord:
Julie's parents
never returned
from that motorcycle
ride.

Those pillows for her resting
after parents' unintended
leave-taking.

Winter Solstice

Brittle glazing on branches,
tilting ground-ward from
blizzard, lists trees as each
dusk edges earlier.
Ancestors' custom of
bonfires, a ritual of
concentrated light
beckoned urgency.
Waning embers' glow
transforms the sodden
and Lenten reserve,
we chose the light.

We Are Driftwood

Inexplicable motion in ebb and flow
ankle-depth urgent waves; we plant
the feet on sand bottom, end-product
of nature, flotsam and drift debris.

Each resistance marks surfaces
in pock, speckle, abrasion,
sculpted contours appear
with each heart-surrender.

Each grace received without
resisting, shirking, or pandering.
Time's journey unspools, freeing
our self-deceits in surrender.

This water and friction mystery
resists or conforms with the driftwood.

PART THREE:

Each Goes It Alone

Solitary We Go	23
Self Exam	24
Rainworks	24
Breathe In and Out	25
Subtraction	26
Easter Ritual	26
Springtime Respite	28
Swallow Darts	28
From That Vantage	29
Dry Spells	29
Weeping Willow	30
Ascendancy	31
Captured Still	32
Boundaries	32
A Hesitation	33
Sketch	34
Submit	34
Attentive	34
Insular	34
Autumnal Angst	35
Jacob's Rod	35
Untitled	36
Gridlock	37
Reluctant Spring	38
Alaskan Sentinels	39

Part Three

Each Goes It Alone

Solitary We Go

No, it's not by two,
halting gait from foot surgery
my pace not hers.

As I continue this marsh trek,
the gap extends, puzzling
how each goes it alone.

Self-Exam

On my best day I'm no gift,
wordsmith spools pretty words,
barbs of self-exiling exude
a smoke screen far and near.

Armadillo-framed mind,
carapace joints, these
platelets, loathing in doubt,
a rancorous shield.

Tipped, underbelly warrants
life-affirming ego-surrender,
we are more than we perceive;
spore with dew in desert.

This couplet, a seedling;
loosen, be chastened, open.

Rainworks

Rhythmic rain patters,
early morning to snuggle
in bed after this drought.

Slumber time invites
forgetfulness in angst
of parched landscapes.

Mind set unlocks as
striated soil wicks
fissures about roots.

Sustained and steady,
a forgiving and forgetting,
soul-soothing respite.

Breathe In and Out

Late January
brisk cold and
atom-connected;
enthralled with
the old magic in
a full moon.

Subtraction

Daffodils and heady hyacinth
punctuate the spring palette;
gather the bouquet.

Disregard; then subtract health,
obligations, entitlements,
regrets, guilt.

Empty. Recalculate the balance:
heart beat with another breath.

Easter Ritual

Humus encapsulates seedling,
leavening to fracture its sheath.

Fibers descend as seismic
ruptures root in the loam.

Within Golgotha, the dark medium,
grain ingests Sun's rays.

Springtime Respite

A mallard hen roosts
on shaded spring grass,
spied from monastery
oratorio, a devotional
beak resting on her body.

Egg clutch and nesting
reinvigorate a Madonna
posturing to be still,
in spite of breeze-
ruffling feathers.

Abrogate busyness;
be still and enter
dormancy; a practice:
seek the quiet.
and contemplate.

Oratorio-a small chapel

Swallow Darts

Fledglings marooned,
fallen from cupped mud
nest, swallows sweep
and swoop the interlopers.

Spying this mishap,
such punishing odds
to ponder.

From That Vantage

Level with second-story window,
camouflaged with leafed branches, a
bird preens its feathers.

Unobserved, free from predator
or immediacy, trunk and wings crimp
and rotate with comfort.

Measure and meditate its
essence, for fly away it will.

Dry Spells

The rain subsides
and earthly humus
exudes all-is-well
freshness.

Rain droplets tumbled,
trickled, recalculating,
regenerating here
calming variances.

Arid horizons
anticipate
reawakening
from dry spells.

Weeping Willows

Jan asked me to take time
and view the golden willows,
glorious, cascading leaves,
suspended fountain heads.

Not unlike minute by minute
passing of days; myopic,
we miss the startle of
wonder all about.

Canadian geese circle
and in v-formation
descend to forage on
shore and gaggle about.
Measures of music, glissandos,
first is attentive quiet.

Beaver Dam Lake

Ascendancy

Gnats and lake fly hatchlings
distract in last May night from
whispery, throaty refrains
of brisk wisps of breeze.

At dusk, a bench with overlook
abandoned, pesky insects,
ephemeral, ascend the moment,
claim our unintended attention.

Captured Still

Hummingbird moth mimicking
avian counterpart extends
nectar-gathering appendage,
sips flower's essence.

Whirring speed dulls its
opaqueness and jewel
luminosity; sustenance
and soul hover all about.

Boundaries

Safflower seed in feeder draws
cardinal mates to roost in the
quarry walls' confines, outstretched
yews and their layering fans.

Vermeil-plumed male
alights and garners quicker
notice than female's more
camouflaged and subdued.

The trill of this song reverberates
ever through seasons, eking
each time from my heart a harmony for
sweet reliance on home boundary.

A Hesitation

Outside the raised kidney-shaped perennial bed
I spot a dander of fluffed strewed grass, a hasty
hutch gathered and formed by rabbit paws and
hind legs excavating into lawn a birthing hole.

Asserting to thwart encroachment my motion
in the fiber is met with feeble mewling of
snuggled and newly born brood; abruptly
I cease from pliant strain of need.

Robert Burns' "To A Mouse" resonates
and through time's unmeasured loop
this chancy hold we share with vulnerable
life companions trumps mindfulness.

Ages hence another more-schooled will
weight Malthusian formula and not hesitate.

Sketch

July leafiness
on sedum hillside as
sumac saplings loft.

Submit

Roadkill sprawled;
not to mind; engage
go with.

Attentive

In this stillness
scarce as any quiet
rain reinvents water.

Insular

Solitary hardwood,
silhouetted waxes
monolithic amid spring-
ready furrows.

Backdrop of near woods
a revel in motion.

Autumnal Angst

Splashes of September light
exacerbate new drought of
leached green thatch.

Curled leaves preclude
autumnal pigmenting,
antiphon for passing fall.

Dies Irae, iridescent
glow foregoes beauteous
blush, unexpected, withheld.

Jacob's Rod

Frost hardy, the perennial does
not wax and wane, ignores freezes;
cajoles me to forestall Josey's Alzheimer's
sentence and intercede for its
stay or commutation.

Steadfast, I anticipate star-shaped
yellow flowers blooming in this
darkening cold season.

Untitled

"Fill the earth and subdue it."
Genesis 1

In this deep-winter
of our quarry-walled yard,
woodchucks again hibernate
below frost line of limestone.

A boundary demarcated; with
spring, trapper sets cages;
terminates unreined appetites
for perennials and rooting.

Imperious to our own
wantonness, this Cain-shadowed
comeuppance expels
such encroachers of Eden.

Boundaries inveigh a realm,
woodchuck, interloper,
is thwarted, for we act
like lethal lesser gods.

Gridlock

"The lives of all men/women we meet and know are woven
in our destiny, together with the lives of many
we shall never know."
Thomas Merton

Fractious Civil War spent,
a muddle of birds peck
at feeders; squawk, jabber
scarcity. Guard territory.

Aren't we above that fray?
Plumage, is not this it?
Song bird or sparrow
vie for seed and suet.

Hunger navigates day
to day flights and roosting,
nesting, preordained
the patterns ensue.

Presages of time, a century
ticked off, await Appomattox.

Reluctant Spring

Heavy and prolonged winter
held all languishing, a sonnet
with third quatrain alludes to
couplet, one's life span.

Anticipated spring, cyclical
protuberances of bulbs, bird banter
greening with Whitman epistle
of grass blade annunciation.

That mystery, seasons, planetary
mechanics, unpredictable this April
with baited cold fronts, heckling
all comes in mindfulness.

Waning years warrant surrender;
seasons intersect the eternal.

Alaskan Sentinels

Smithsonian permanent loan
of first nation Eskimo, Aleut,
and Indian artifacts radiate from
exhibits in a cathedral aura.

Intact beading, a braille for
awe of flora and fauna, on
hide and pelt, stitched, fabricated
as vestments in sacred rite.

Latitude infringes on light;
inner eye resurrects intricacy
with such delicacy and variety of
in these abbreviated seasons.

Circle of life and death,
seal, caribou, bear, eagle,
millennial song and dance,
reverberating in this moment.

                                      Tour of Anchorage Museum

"It is difficult
to get news from poems
yet men die miserably every day
for lack
of what is found there."

-William Carlos Williams

www.ingramcontent.com/pod-product-compliance
Lightning Source LLC
Chambersburg PA
CBHW040331300426
44113CB00020B/2722